LIBRARY
COLLEGE OF THE REDWOODS
EUREKA, CALIFORNIA 95501

D1773318

OVERSIZE   67550
F
882
C63
W37
1979

Watkins, Carleton Emmons
Photographs of the Columbia River
and Oregon

LIBRARY
COLLEGE OF THE REDWOODS
EUREKA, CALIFORNIA 95501

CARLETON E. WATKINS

PHOTOGRAPHS OF THE COLUMBIA RIVER AND OREGON

EDITED BY JAMES ALINDER WITH ESSAYS BY DAVID FEATHERSTONE AND RUSS ANDERSON

THE FRIENDS OF PHOTOGRAPHY IN ASSOCIATION WITH THE WESTON GALLERY

© 1979, The Friends of Photography, Inc.

All rights reserved in all countries. No part of this book may be reproduced or translated in any form without written permission from The Friends of Photography, except for brief passages which may be quoted in a review.

Library of Congress Catalogue Card No. 79-54978
ISBN #0-933286-13-9 (clothbound); #0-933286-14-7 (paperbound)

PREFACE

History is much more fluid, and its recording much less complete, than we have tended to realize. The gaps in our information about the history of photography are enormous. Our understanding of the medium has, in large part, come from only a half-dozen writers whose achievements, while awesome, are not encyclopedic. As knowledge inevitably expands there will be a continued refinement of the merits ascribed to individual photographers. This book is evidence of that ongoing process as it presents the photographs of a remarkable artist whose work has commanded scant attention over the past century.

Recent historical discoveries and reassessments have come about not only through increased intellectual interest but through a burgeoning demand for 19th century photographs. With as much perspective as the last year of the decade allows, it is apparent that during the 1970s photography's position as a collectible art medium solidified. While certain museums had begun collections of photography far earlier, this decade saw hundreds of previously reticent museums, as well as corporations and individuals, enter the market in serious ways. To accommodate this increased demand the search for pictures from photography's first century was undertaken in earnest. One conspicuous result has been the discovery of additional bodies of strong work leading to the reevaluation of the importance of several photographers. These reassessments are being forced not only because of increased knowledge about the photographer's *oeuvre,* but by changed judgments of contemporary taste as to what we believe to be important art.

Certainly no critical reevaluation is more justified than the elevation of Carleton E. Watkins to a position of significance. From a little-known photographer not even mentioned in Beaumont Newhall's revised and enlarged edition of the standard history of the medium, Watkins has, in the judgement of many, emerged as the most important single American photographer before Alfred Stieglitz.

Until recently there was only one known album containing the photographs reproduced in this book—that in the Bender Rare Book Room of the Stanford University Library. A second album, and the one which was used to make the plates for this book, was discovered recently on the bottom shelf of the library at The University Club in New York City. Representatives of The Swann Galleries of New York came across the album during a commissioned appraisal of the Club's holdings. Realizing, albeit to a limited extent, the rarity and value of the pictures as works of art, the Club decided to sell the album, along with another Watkins album of views of the Pacific Coast, to augment its operating funds.

News of the discovery of the Watkins albums, and their potential availability, spread through an inner circle of curators, collectors and dealers. Weston Naef, of New York's prestigious Metropolitan Museum, made a strong effort to acquire both albums for the Museum's collection. To assure fairness in the sale of the albums as well as to receive a potentially higher price, however, The University Club decided against a private sale and asked the Swann Galleries to sell the albums at a public auction. A estimated price of $5,000 was initially established, but that was raised to a range of $20,000 to $30,000 per album by the time the auction catalogue was published.

The albums were auctioned on Thursday, May 10, 1979, in several minutes of stunning bidding during which the albums made history as the most expensive photographic properties ever sold at auction. The *Pacific Coast* album of 49 mammoth plate prints (20¾ x 15¾ inches) went to the Hastings Galleries of New York and fetched $98,000. The 51 mammoth plates of the *Columbia River and Oregon* album came to The Weston Gallery of Carmel for $100,000.

When Margaret W. Weston, owner of The Weston Gallery, returned from the auction I approached her with the idea that The Friends of Photography hold an exhibition of the prints from the Watkins album and publish them as a book. Feeling responsible for repositing with history the full sense of the album before the individual plates were sold, Weston readily agreed to both projects. We also agreed that three other conditions were necessary to serve this magnificent art: that all 51 of the plates in the album be exhibited and published, that they be in the exact order which Watkins established and that the printing of the book be a state-of-the-art production.

I discussed the printing aspect of the Watkins project with David Gardner of Gardner/Fulmer Lithograph of Buena Park, California. Gardner's enthusiasm for the project grew rapidly and his preliminary sets of press proofs were convincing to me. The proofs which most accurately replicated the feeling of the original prints were from negatives exposed on the laser scanner and printed by a three color process. Since the reproductions in this book are only one-fourth as large as the actual mammoth plate contact prints, nothing less than the finest rendering of tone and detail would do justice to the originals.

The task of writing an historical article on Watkins with emphasis on the Oregon expedition during which these photographs were made was given to David Featherstone, Executive Assistant of The Friends. His interest in Watkins, his knowledge of Oregon and his clear and perceptive writing made him the perfect choice. Featherstone's study of Watkins' life began in 1974 while he was working as Curator of Historical Photographs at the University of Oregon Library in Eugene. His research expanded two years later and became intensive in preparing the article for this book.

To clarify details of Watkins' trip, Featherstone returned to Oregon both to research historical collections in the state and to reexperience the area in which Watkins worked. He also visited institutions in California to search for primary sources. Featherstone was able to discover a number of previously unknown facts—even proving that Watkins' expedition to Oregon was in 1867, not 1868, as had been believed. The 1868 date had been routinely accepted because it was included in a 1918 narrative written by historian Charles

Turrill, who collected information from an ailing Watkins in the years before the photographer's death. Turrill's report is now known to contain a number of inaccuracies. Featherstone's remarkable elucidation of the events surrounding Watkins' travels in Oregon and along the Columbia River should be seen as part of the untangling of the history of photography. It is an extension of the recent serious investigations of Watkins' life and work published by Pauline Grenbeaux, Peter Palmquist and Nanette Sexton in the Fall, 1978, issue of *California History*.

If historical efforts have been limited, scholarly critical examination of the monumental artistic achievements of Carleton E. Watkins has been almost nonexistent. The photographs in the *Columbia River and Oregon* album present a fine opportunity to study a body of work closely and to glean a richer appreciation of Watkins' power as a picture maker. Russ Anderson made such a study and wrote an illuminating critical essay for this book. Anderson is the Associate Director and 19th Century Specialist at The Weston Gallery, a position he accepted after having been a photography dealer in London from 1973 to 1978. Anderson's additional critical interests include P.H. Emerson and early photography in Britain and France. In his perceptive article Anderson traces a growing quality of abstraction in Watkins' work of this period. He discusses several prints in depth, clarifying their nature as individual pictures. Anderson also identifies the remarkable serial development of Watkins' pictorial motifs.

I am grateful to many people whose contributions have made the publication of this book possible. I would like to express my sincere thanks to Margaret W. Weston for making the album available; to David Featherstone and Russ Anderson not only for their essays but for additional help along the way; to Weston Naef for his early championing of Watkins, in part through his 1975 book, *Era of Exploration;* to David Gardner and the staff at Gardner/Fulmer Lithograph for making the reproductions glow on the page; and to George Stimson for his technical photographic assistance.

For their cooperation and assistance in the publication of this book I am most grateful to Mr. & Mrs. Ansel Adams, Mr. & Mrs. Leonard Vernon, Dr. & Mrs. Gerson Lesnick and Mr. & Mrs. Charles Boxenbaum. Sincere thanks also go to Cindy Moffitt for her able research assistance throughout the project, to the staff of the various institutions whose collections were consulted—particularly to Edward Kemp, Elaine Kemp and Phil Zorich of the University of Oregon Library, Susan Seyl and Paul E. Ewing III of the Oregon Historical Society, Suzanne Gallup of the Bancroft Library, Glenn Mason of the Lane County Pioneer Museum and Glenn Hartwell and John Webb of the Oregon State Library—and to Shirley Freemesser and David Turner for their bibliographic assistance.

For their editorial help thanks go to Robert Baker, Andrea Turnage, Mary Alinder, Pauline Grenbeaux and Peter Palmquist. Thanks are also due to Tricia Doran and Nancy Ponedel, who typed the manuscripts; to Suzie Frerkson, who set it in Garamond type; and to Peter A. Andersen, whose clean design makes the book even more beautiful.

It is a particular pleasure for The Friends of Photography, often identified with the more contemporary aspects of the medium, to present, in association with The Weston Gallery, this collection of photographs. Rather than having an extremely limited public view, the *Columbia River and Oregon* album is preserved in this publication and for the first time thousands will be able to enjoy the remarkably contemporary and austere lyricism of the photographs of Carleton E. Watkins.

James Alinder, Editor

CARLETON E. WATKINS

THE COLUMBIA RIVER AND OREGON EXPEDITION

by David Featherstone

Carleton Watkins' position as a preeminent photographer of the American West is undisputed. Details of his activities have long eluded researchers, however, because the hard evidence of his active years was lost first in a bankruptcy in the 1870s and even more disastrously in the fire following the 1906 San Francisco earthquake. The record of Watkins' arrival in California in the early 1850s is unclear, but his move was made as a part of a sustained migration of Oneonta, New York, residents who, like people from all areas of the East, traveled west following the discovery of gold in the hills of California.

Carleton E. Watkins was born in Oneonta on November 11, 1829, the youngest of five children.[1] His Scottish parents were the proprietors of Angell's Hotel in Oneonta. The hotel was a frequent stopping place for Collis P. Huntington, a young hardware salesman who was to become one of the principal builders of the Central Pacific Railroad and a long-time patron of Watkins in his career as a photographer. The precise date of Watkins' move west has not been established, although there is a C. Watkins on the passenger list of the Michaelangelo, a ship which arrived in San Francisco from New York on August 2, 1852.[2] It is known that by 1853 Watkins had settled in Sacramento where he worked as a carpenter and lived in the home of G. W. Murray, a book-seller and stationer from Oneonta who had been the bookkeeper for Huntington's hardware company there.

Watkins followed Murray to San Francisco in late 1853, and is listed in the 1854 city directory as a clerk in Murray's store. It was during this period that Watkins began his career in photography as a camera operator for Robert Vance. Vance was a daguerreotypist who had galleries in Sacramento, where Watkins probably first met him, and San Jose, as well as in San Francisco. Vance apparently hired Watkins, who knew nothing about the daguerreotype process, to replace temporarily an operator in his San Jose gallery. Vance was to go to his southern studio as soon as possible to retake the portraits which would surely be done poorly by the neophyte daguerreotypist. Watkins took to the process immediately, however, and Vance kept him on as an operator in the San Jose studio. This account of Watkins' initial success seems to be an example of romanticized history and it is likely that the actual events did not transpire so fluidly. Watkins' career had begun, however, and he remained in San Jose for several years working for Vance and, later, as manager of the San Jose outlet of Ford's Daguerrean Gallery.

Charles B. Turrill, Watkins' biographer, reports that the photographer returned to San Francisco in 1857 or early 1858,[3] but his name does not appear in the city directories of those years. In 1861 he is listed as a "daguerrean operator" at 425 Montgomery Street, a term which implies that he either worked for another photographer or on a free-lance basis.

Competition among commercial galleries was keen during the 1850s and early 1860s. Portraits formed the bulk of the business for most photographers, who provided likenesses of their customers first with daguerreotypes and ambrotypes and, beginning in the 1860s, with tintypes and small albumen paper prints mounted as cartes-de-visite. Larger portraits were possible but these small prints were by far the most popular.

Photographs of non-portrait subjects were made, of course, even though they were not as commercially viable as portraits. Watkins' mentor, Robert Vance, exhibited a collection of 300 whole-plate daguerreotypes of California scenes in New York as early as 1851. It was not until the development of wet plate collodion negatives and albumen prints, which allowed photographers to make multiple prints from a single negative, that the expense of extended travel away from the studio could be recouped through sales of prints.

The stereograph—first produced as glass transparencies, then as paper prints mounted on cards—was also gaining popularity during the late 1850s. It was, in fact, the stereograph which provided photographers in the West with their most profitable market. These technical developments, combined with the desire of those still in the East to learn about the land in which their friends and relatives were living, helped establish the market for landscape photographs. The era of expeditionary wet-plate photography in the West began.

Much has been made of the difficulties encountered by photographers using the wet plate process in the field. Once the camera was set up at a site to be photographed, the photographer prepared his plate in a portable dark tent, carefully coating a sheet of glass with the collodion mixture and sensitizing it with a solution of silver nitrate. The plate was then placed in a negative holder and inserted in the camera. After the several-second exposure was made it was necessary to develop the image in the dark tent before the light-sensitive emulsion dried. The problems inherent in the process, all enormously magnified when extremely large sheets of glass were used, ranged from spilled chemicals and uneven application of the solutions to light leaks and the stifling heat created in a small dark tent set up in the summer's heat. It should be remembered, however, that mid-19th century photographers accepted these inconveniences not as limitations but as characteristics inherent to the process of photography.

Watkins did venture with his camera into the countryside while in San Jose, but his first extensive photographic trip was in 1859, when he visited the Mariposa area just west of Yosemite. The Mariposa photographs, the earliest body of Watkins' photographs known,[4] were commissioned for use in an article included in the July, 1859, issue of *Hutchings California Magazine*. The imperial-sized photographs, approximately 13½ x 16 inches, were used as models by the artists who made the wood-cut engravings actually printed in the magazine.[5] Following the practice of the time, no credit was given to the photographer.

James M. Hutchings, editor and publisher of the magazine, must be acknowledged for the role he played in leading photographers into the rural areas of California. During the same summer he sent Watkins to Mariposa he also commissioned another San Francisco photographer, C.L. Weed, to accompany him on a trip to Yosemite Valley.[6] Like Watkins, Weed was an early employee of Vance. He had been manager of Vance's Sacramento gallery, but moved to San Francisco in early 1859 to help his employer refurbish the gallery there which had been destroyed by fire the previous summer.

Typically, Hutchings' commission did not preclude Weed's using any of the photographs made in Yosemite for his own purposes. Within a few days after his return to San Francisco forty stereo views from the trip were put on display in Vance's gallery. It was this group of photographs, along with some twenty 11 x 14-inch views, which probably triggered Watkins' desire to go to Yosemite himself.

Like all photographers of the period, Watkins was anxious to surpass his competition. He wanted not only to be able to offer photographs of the same locations as other photographers, but to make them better. In this era before enlargements could be made easily from small negatives, prints were contact-printed from a negative of equal size. A large negative was necessary in order to produce a large print. Since photographers using the wet-plate process were not bound by the "standard" sizes later imposed by commercial film manufacturers, a camera could be made to any size desired. Watkins had one built that held 18 x 22-inch plates and it was this giant wooden box that he took to Yosemite in 1861.

Extremely large cameras such as Watkins' were not unknown in 1860, even though the vast majority of photographs made were considerably smaller. Despite the expense of the large glass and the amounts of chemicals which the oversized negatives required, the finely-detailed grandeur of the resulting prints could not be denied. By the late 1850s a number of photographers, primarily in England and France, were using the wet plate process with large scale cameras. In 1855 Edouard Baldus made his famous railway series using plates 14 x 21 inches. The same year Roger Fenton traveled in the Crimea using cameras of a variety of sizes, but by the end of the decade he worked extensively with a 15 x 18-inch camera. During the same period Francis Frith carried his mammoth plate camera on three trips to the Middle East. By 1860, however, European interest in the oversized photograph seems to have waned and the province of the mammoth plate camera shifted to the United States.

In retrospect, Watkins' use of the mammoth camera seems to be the major achievement of his 1861 Yosemite trip, but it was the stereographs he made that summer, rather than the large prints, which brought his initial acclaim as a landscape photographer. They also probably formed the greater part of his commercial sales from the expedition. In a successful attempt at self-promotion Watkins sent a selection of his glass stereographs to the writer and photographic enthusiast, Oliver Wendell Holmes. Holmes commented favorably on them in an article published in 1863 in the *Atlantic Monthly*.

> One of the most interesting accessions to our collection is a series of twelve views, on glass, of scenes and objects in California, sent us with unprovoked liberality by the artist, Mr. Watkins. As specimens of art they are admirable, and some of the subjects are among the most interesting to be found in the whole realm of Nature. Thus, the great tree, the "Grizzly Giant" of Mariposa, is shown in two admirable views; the mighty precipice of El Capitan, more than 3,000 feet in precipitious height, and three conical hill tops of Yosemite, taken not as they soar into the atmosphere, but as they are reflected in the calm waters below—these and others are shown, clear, yet soft, vigorous in the foreground, delicately distinct in the distance, in a perfection of art which compares with the finest European work.[7]

As Watkins' reputation as a photographer of landscape was beginning to take hold he exhibited his Yosemite photographs at galleries in other parts of the country, including the prestigious Goupil's Gallery in New York and W. T. Shanahan's music store and gallery in Portland, Oregon. He used his large camera to photograph San Francisco and the central California coast as far north as Mendocino, but he gained prominence as a photographer of Yosemite. He returned there in 1864 as a photographer for the survey team led by J. D. Whitney and again in both 1865 and 1866.

The degree of success Watkins enjoyed by 1867 is indicated by his sudden flurry of professional activities. In the 1867 San Francisco city directory he identified himself for the first time as a "landscape photographer". In the early part of that year he opened the Yosemite Art Gallery at his 425 Montgomery Street address. The name given the gallery was an obvious attempt not only to capitalize on the subject matter for which he was becoming known, but also to wrest public identification with Yosemite away from his growing competition. As a further sign of his commercial maturity he assured control of his work by establishing copyright of his photographs and published his stereographs on cards bearing the general title "Watkins' Pacific Coast". The copyright notice, title and file number of each photograph were printed on the face of the card; an advertisement for the Yosemite Art Gallery on the reverse.

Watkins' most significant undertaking of 1867, however, and one which becomes more remarkable considering the demands which must have been made on him by his new gallery, was his nearly four-month trip to Oregon and the Columbia River. He surely recognized that for his new gallery to succeed it would be necessary for him to add significantly to his catalogue of photographs. It is a sign of his early desire to market only his own work that he chose to travel away from his gallery rather than employing others to make photographs for him as many photographers did.

With the entire western portion of the continent open to him and virtually unphotographed, it is reasonable to ask why Watkins chose to make his first major trip out of central California as far away as the Columbia River. It must be remembered, however, that although the California gold rush hastened settlement of that state, Spanish control of the area had limited its accessibility for those in the East before 1845. The Oregon Territory had become part of the United States some four decades earlier. After the preliminary explorations of Meriwether Lewis and William Clark, who traveled through the Oregon Territory between 1804 and 1806, the Northwest was etched into the consciousness of the young country as the gateway to the Pacific Ocean. Watkins would have assimilated this awareness while a boy in New York. Considering his obvious interest in exhibiting and selling his photographs in the East and the existence of an established outlet in Portland, it is really not surprising that he chose to travel to Oregon.

Watkins arrived in Portland during mid-July, 1867, aboard the *Oriflamme*, a steamer which regularly made the four-day run from San Francisco.[8] Although he is not listed among the passengers who arrived on July 12, a short notice printed three days later in the Portland *Oregonian* suggests that he had come on the most recent boat.

VISIT FROM AN ARTIST. Mr. C.E. Watkins, a gentleman who has been for some time engaged in taking photographic views of notable places in California, came passenger on the *Oriflamme* and goes up the Columbia this morning for the purpose of taking observations from various points preparatory to photographing Mt. Hood. In the course of a brief call upon us yesterday, he informed us that he intends to take views wherever he may find the scenery remarkable. He ascended to the summits of two or three of the hills west of this city yesterday, and says that the view from the summit of Robinson Hill is the most variedly picturesque that he ever saw— combining as it does, in one view, the city, many miles of both the Willamette and Columbia rivers, with their confluence and the majestic flow of the Columbia, thence, oceanward, forests, plains, the dark blue range of the Cascades, with every snow peak in full view from Diamond Peak in Southern Oregon, to Mt. Baker, near the British Columbia border. Mr.

Watkins will return from the Cascades this evening and enter immediately upon preparations for the prosecution of his work. There are several of his pictures of California scenery on exhibition and for sale in this city. Mr. Shanahan has some of them framed and hung against the walls of his art gallery, corner of Front and Morrison Streets.

By his visit to the newspaper office, an act of self-promotion similar to his sending the Yosemite stereographs to Oliver Wendell Holmes several years earlier, Watkins not only renewed public awareness of his previous work but assured interest when the results of his trip were displayed later in Portland. W. T. Shanahan, who owned the music store and gallery where Watkins had his photographs on display, was a former resident of San Francisco who may have had some influence on the photographer's decision to make the trip to Oregon. Shanahan's advertisement in the 1867 city directory gave notice of his carrying "views of Columbia River scenery". Although these may have been paintings rather than photographs, it is significant that a local market for imagery of the Columbia River did exist at the time of Watkins' visit.

Watkins was, of course, not the first photographer to work in the Portland area; the development of photography there paralleled that in other cities in the West. The first photographers in the area were traveling daguerreotypists who would spend a few days making portraits in one community before moving on to the next. The earliest record of these itinerant photographers in Oregon is the newspaper notice of a Mr. Jennings who, on January 30, 1851, urged the citizens of Oregon City to "secure the shadow ere the substance fades".[9] Two years later L. H. Wakefield opened the first permanent daguerreotype studio in Portland, but it was another 1853 entrant into the field, Joseph Buchtel, who was to become the best known of the city's early photographers. Over the next decade he moved his gallery a number of times, always keeping it in the center of the expanding Portland business area. By 1867 he had settled on the corner of First and Morrison, a block from the Shanahan gallery. Although portraits formed the major portion of his work, Buchtel had a rare sense of history which led him, after the introduction of the wet plate process, not only to keep all of his glass negatives, despite the expense of the glass, but to maintain an alphabetical list of subjects. During the summer of 1867 Buchtel ran a daily advertisement in the *Oregonian* declaring his gallery to be the only one in Oregon "thoroughly prepared to do all the different styles of work in the art".

Although the *Oregonian* notice on July 15 made direct reference to photographing Mt. Hood, it is curious that Watkins did not actually photograph the mountain except as a part of a distant horizon. Mt. Hood forms a commanding part of the view from Portland, rising some 10,000 feet above the town. Wagon roads would have provided easy access to the southern approach to the mountain with considerably less effort than was required for Watkins' previous expeditions along the rim of Yosemite Valley. Once traveling along the Columbia, Watkins would have discovered that the mountain was hidden from view by the steep gorge which formed when the Columbia cut its way through the Cascade Range.

The "Cascades" mentioned in the newspaper article which Watkins was to visit on July 15 was not the mountain range but, rather, a section of rapids on the Columbia some forty miles upstream from Portland. During the mid-19th century the Columbia River played an immensely important role in the economic development of the Northwest. It was navigable for several hundred miles from its mouth at Astoria, with the exception of a few stretches of treacherous rapids. One of these was at Cascades, where a six-mile portage was necessary before river travel was again possible. Obviously, control of travel on the river was an economic advantage and by 1867 the Oregon Steam Navigation Company (OSNC) had established a transportation monopoly, owning the river boats as well as the portage railways.

Figure 1.

It is not possible to determine the day to day movement of Watkins in Oregon and along the Columbia River, but the sequencing he established when the mammoth plate prints and stereographs were published provides a clue. It was Watkins' practice to number each subject category beginning with an even hundred, allowing him to add subsequent pictures in a logical position within his catalogue. The mammoth plate Oregon pictures were numbered beginning with 400; the stereographs with 1200. The photograph collection at the Oregon Historical Society in Portland contains a large group of prints made from the 18 x 22-inch negatives, mounted on boards with a printed copyright notice. There is also a hand-written number on the mount just below the lower right corner of the print. The trip described by the sequence of these numbers—from Portland south to Oswego and Oregon City, then along the Columbia River from Portland to Celilo, some 100 miles upstream—is matched by that of the 136 stereocards Watkins also published following his trip. Recognizing that the photographs may not have been made precisely in this order, the sequence does provide a convincing framework for describing his trip.

If Watkins did actually make the investigatory trip up the Columbia on July 15th, he began his picture-making back in Portland. On July 20th the *Oregonian* reported him still in the hills above the town, waiting for an unseasonal mid-summer storm to clear.

> WAITING TO TAKE A PICTURE. Mr. Watkins, the celebrated photographist of scenery, has his instruments in readiness on the summit of the hill adjoining Robinson's Hill, on the south, to take a view of Mt. Hood and the surrounding scenery, whenever the weather will permit. Ever since his arrival here we have had almost continuous bad weather for the taking of such pictures.

The weather did finally clear and Watkins made a three-part panoramic view of Portland and the surrounding area. The evidence of the rain which delayed his photographs is present in the near flood-stage of the Willamette River. Mt. Hood appears faintly in the distance in the right hand panel, dwarfed by the 70-degree angle of view of Watkins' lens.[10] These photographs do not match the view described in the July 15 *Oregonian* article. Even though distant peaks would have been obscured because of the extra blue sensitivity of Watkins' plates,

Figure 1. City of Portland and the Willamette River (see Plates 1 & 2). Right panel of panorama courtesy of the Oregon Historical Society, Portland.

Figure 2. The Oregon Iron Company at Oswego (see Plates 12 & 13).

Figure 3. Oregon City & Willamette Falls (see Plates 4, 5 & 6).

Figure 2.

the hyperbolic newspaper description—the view contained in the 500 miles between Mt. Baker and Diamond Peak would have been remarkable even in pre-pollution days—was likely the chauvinistic invention of the editors.

The Portland panorama and the two others present among the Oregon photographs are interesting because there is no evidence that Watkins had attempted similar multi-part photographs previously. During his 1866 Yosemite trip he did make several photographs from Sentinel Dome which survey the landscape, but the overlap between them is great and they do not appear to be intended as one unit. The care taken in making the Oregon panoramas is astonishing; the overlap between the 22-inch wide plates is as small as one-sixteenth inch. The 66-inch panoramas, which Watkins mounted within a single frame, made an impressive display.[11]

It is interesting to note that while all three sections of the Portland panorama are in the collection of the Oregon Historical Society, only two were included when the presentation album *Photographs of the Columbia River and Oregon* was made in the early 1870s (Plates 1 and 2.) Breakage of fragile glass negatives, a constant problem for all glass plate photographers, was even more critical for those using mammoth plates. It is likely that the third negative did not survive the years between the first publication of the photographs and the preparation of the albums.

From Portland Watkins traveled upstream along the Willamette River to Oswego, where he photographed the buildings of the Oregon Iron Company.[12] Among the photographs he made there is a two-panel panorama with connections between the parts so subtle that they are easily missed (Plates 12 and 13). The rutted, brush-covered foreground and the dissimilar buildings in the prints provide little suggestions that the two can be joined. It is only the corner of the building in the left panel extending into the edge of the right-hand print which makes the connection clear. The individual parts were designed with a structural integrity which allows them to stand alone while contributing to the larger panoramic image.

Throughout his career Watkins had an eye for subject matter that was newsworthy and, thus, salable. As early as 1857, while still in San Jose, he photographed the New Almaden Quicksilver Mine at a time when the owners of the mine were involved in a lawsuit over conflicting land claims. Turrill points out that Watkins "received quite an incentive in

Figure 3.

his photographic career from the sale of pictures" of the mine because of the attention given to the case in the press.[13] Similar motivations must have been behind Watkins' photographs of the Oregon Iron Company, which was the first plant on the Pacific Coast to manufacture pig iron in a blast furnace. The plant began production on August 24, 1867, and it is clear that Watkins was in Oswego shortly before that time. The factory buildings are new and there is evidence of construction still in progress. Stacks of wood to fire the furnace surround the main building in Plate 14. If the Oswego pictures were not commissioned by the owners of the Iron Company, and there is no evidence that they were, Watkins surely realized that sales of the pictures would be possible once the company's impact on the Pacific Coast economy was realized.

Watkins continued south six miles to Oregon City, the first capital of the state. The Willamette Falls at Oregon City represented the same navigational barrier as the Cascades on the Columbia. A portage around the falls allowed river travel from Portland to cities along the Willamette as far upstream as Eugene, a distance of 170 river miles. The industries that grew up around the falls—transportation, boat building and the flour, woolen and paper mills which depended on the falls for power—reflected the key position of the city.

From the site of Linn City, on the west bank of the river, Watkins produced a three-part panorama *Oregon City and the Willamette Falls* (Plates 4, 5 & 6). Plate 7, made from the same camera position, continues the view to include the entire falls area, but the duplication with Plate 6 is so great that it appears to have been conceived as a separate view. As with the previous panoramas, the overlap between sections is extremely small. This panorama is perhaps more interesting than the others because of the richness of the information it contains. The left-hand panel (Plate 4) shows the town and the steamboat docks below the falls. The large brick building to the right of the frame, which still stands today although surrounded by a large paper mill, was the home of the Oregon Woolen Mills. The center panel (Plate 5) shows the Imperial Flour Mill and the dock area above the falls as well as an unusual drydock arrangement at the crest of the falls. The right-hand panel (Plate 6) continues the view of the falls itself, with the smoothness of the water indicating that an exposure of several seconds was necessary for the large glass plates.

After completing his work along the Willamette River Watkins returned to Portland to prepare for his trip along the

Columbia, possibly storing his completed negatives at the Shanahan gallery. The first photograph he made after leaving Portland for the second phase of his summer's travels was a distant view of Mt. Hood (Plate 15), taken from the Washington State side of the Columbia, near Vancouver.

Watkins may have traveled on the Oregon Steam Navigation Company boat making its regular run up the river—the first stop after leaving Portland was Vancouver—but he more likely traveled in the smaller sailing craft which appears in later pictures (Plates 16, 17).

The photographs Watkins made along the Columbia River are tied so closely to the operations of the OSNC that the possibility of an official relationship between Watkins and the transportation company is intriguing. The numbers on the published stereocards and mammoth prints directly correspond with the geographic sequence of locations along the river which the traveler would see on the trip from Portland to Celilo. Many of the photographs Watkins made along the Columbia River were of the buildings and other facilities of the OSNC and all of the exposures were made within a few yards of the water's edge. Significantly, a number of sights not visible from the river, but which Watkins could have reached without difficulty, including a stream, gorge and waterfall bearing the name of his home town in New York, were not photographed.

One reason sponsorship of the 1867 trip may be suspected is that, throughout his career, much of Watkins' travel was directly connected with survey projects or with the railroads. In 1864 and 1866 he photographed in Yosemite with John Whitney's survey teams. In 1870 he worked with the U.S. Geological Survey in the Mount Shasta and Mount Lassen areas of Northern California. In 1873 he traveled to Utah with painter William Keith along the Union Pacific Railroad and in 1880 he made an extended trip through Southern California and Arizona, photographing along the Southern Pacific routes.

His first trip to Yosemite, in 1861, was apparently made on his own, however, so a precedent for a purely speculative Oregon trip does exist. Watkins may have felt that the importance of the Oregon Steam Navigation Company to the developing Northwest economy would help create a market for his photographs, in Portland as well as in other cities. The transportation monopoly was not unknown in California; in 1867 the first shipments of wheat were made to San Francisco through the OSNC network by farmers who lived upstream from the Cascades.

Even if there was no direct support of his travels, an informal relationship between Watkins and the OSNC should not be ruled out. The owners might have willingly offered the courtesies of passage and lodging, recognizing that distribution of the photographs Watkins made, even general views of the landscape, would extend the reputation of the company so closely identified with the Columbia River.

At the site of this first Columbia River photograph Watkins also made a stereograph, moving slightly closer so that the fence posts in the field would become a foreground element in the stereo. Throughout his travels in Oregon Watkins used his stereo camera considerably more often than he did the mammoth plate camera, finishing the trip with 57 large negatives and 136 stereographs.[14] Obviously less expensive to operate, the smaller camera could also be manipulated more easily in difficult situations. Almost all of the mammoth views are matched by a stereocard made, if not from the same location, from a nearby vantage point. The panorama of Portland is accompanied by a 9-part stereo sequence which covers the same area; the Oregon City-Willamette Falls panorama by a six-stereograph group. When the stereo exposure was made from a different location than the mammoth view, as was the case along the river near Vancouver, it was generally done so that foreground objects could be incorporated to accentuate the feeling of deep space which was part of the visual appeal of the stereograph.

The photograph of Rooster Rock, on the Oregon side of the river (Plate 16) demonstrates that the mammoth views and the stereographs were made as a part of the same photographic effort. The photographer's dark tent is seen in the distance, in front of the trees. With aid of a magnifying glass a tripod is visible next to the tent. To the right of the picture, next to the large tree, a stereo camera is set up. Watkins rarely allowed evidence of the process of photography to appear in his photographs and the inclusion of the camera and dark tent here is unusual. Comparative analysis of Plate 16 and the Watkins Stereograph No. 1228 reveals that the stereo was not made from precisely the camera position shown in the mammoth photograph. The shifting of the shadow of the large tree from one picture to the other indicates that the stereo was made several minutes after the large view.

From Rooster Rock Watkins crossed the river to Cape Horn (Plates 17, 18 and 48), an impressive rock formation jutting into the river from the Washington side. It is known that the photographer's guide on the Columbia River portion of his trip was a man named John W. Stevenson.[15] The Stevenson family was the first to settle in the Cape Horn area and owned the property there which was used as a boat landing. Stevenson's sister was the wife of Joseph Bailey, operator of the Oregon Portage Railroad at Eagle Creek, a part of the Oregon Steam Navigation Company system.[16]

The two cases of apples which appear in Plate 17 are explained by the presence of the Stevenson family property at Cape Horn. Strange supplies for a photography trip, the apples were probably being delivered to or shipped from the family farm. What is significant in the photograph, however, is the stack of crates on the beach. With a magnifying glass it is possible to make out the inscription on the box immediately underneath the apples. The label is that of Weatherford Drugs, a Portland store located very near the Shanahan gallery which advertised that it carried chemicals and window glass as well as regular drug items. The size and number of the boxes in the photograph suggest that Watkins did not return to Portland during the Columbia River trip, but carried sufficient supplies for its duration.

Multnomah Falls, on the Oregon side of the river, was the next stop on the trip upstream. The falls, which drops more than 600 feet from the wall of the Columbia Gorge, must have intrigued Watkins because of its similarity to the two-stage Yosemite Falls. He made three mammoth views of the falls (Plates 49-51), along with six stereographs. Note should be made here of the sequencing of the reproductions in this book, which follows exactly that of the presentation album which contained the originals. The three Multnomah Falls photographs, all vertical in format, plus an additional vertical view of Cape Horn (Plate 48), were placed at the rear of the album. Since with a few exceptions the general sequence of the album follows that of both the published mammoth views and stereocards, it appears that the vertical photographs were placed together to facilitate viewing the prints. The entire album weighed in excess of 60 pounds and would have been awkward to view had the verticals been placed in their normal sequence.

Continuing up the river, past Castle Rock, a monolith rising some 750 feet above the river on the Washington side, Watkins reached the Cascades area of the Columbia. Within that six-mile stretch he made twenty mammoth views and 58 stereographs. Since the entire area is now under water, flooded in 1938 after the completion of the Bonneville Dam, this group of photographs provides an important and valuable historical record.

What is significant in the photographs made in the Cascades is the ease with which Watkins moved between documents of the Oregon Steam Navigation Company facilities along the river and photographs of pure landscape. He confronted both types of subjects throughout his career, of course. The attention given the early Yosemite photographs, however, which contain little evidence of human presence, has led to Watkins' modern reputation as a photographer of untrampled landscape. In his book *Era of Exploration* Weston

Naef considers Watkins a photographer of pure landscape influenced by the almost spiritual interest in nature which was current during the mid-19th century.[17] This influence was certainly present, and Naef's conclusion might be appropriate if only the Yosemite work is considered. The Oregon photographs are generally indicative of the breadth of Watkins' photographic interests, however. It is clear that the photographer was as concerned with the interaction between man and the environment as he was with wilderness landscape. In business to sell photographs, he turned his camera to whatever subjects he thought would have a commercial market.

Watkins must have spent a number of days in the Cascades area. By 1867 tracks for the portage railroad had been built along both sides of the river and access to many locations would have been easy. With several trains going each direction daily connecting the steamboats on either end of the Cascades, he would have been able to spend several hours—or days—at one location, then catch a ride to the next. That he did not travel with just one train, using it repeatedly in the photographs, can be seen by comparing the mammoth print *The Collapsed High Bridge* (Plate 27) with the stereograph made of the same subject. The stereo camera was set up in the same place as the larger one, but the engine stopped on the tracks when the stereo exposure was made had no cars attached to it.

The seven photographs made at Upper Cascades, where passengers and freight were transferred from trains back to steamboats to continue the trip toward Dalles City, illustrate the depth of Watkins' interest in the Oregon Steam Navigation Company (Plates 28-34). In these photographs he thoroughly covered the area, almost excessively considering the lack of such duplication within the rest of his Columbia River and Oregon work. Plates 28 and 29 are views made in opposition to each other—Plate 29 taken from a point near the tall tree in Plate 28, the latter taken just above the joining of the tracks on the western end of the bridges. Given Watkins' obvious attraction to this area, it is curious that he did not make a multi-plate panoramic view of the Upper Cascades as he did of Portland and Oregon City. The series *Islands in the Columbia* (Plates 31-33) present different aspects of a contiguous area, but the camera position was changed for each exposure and there was no attempt to join the images.

After making the photographs of Upper Cascades, Watkins moved across the river to the site of the Oregon Portage Railroad, the earliest of the portage railroads along the Columbia (Plates 36 and 37). Built in the early 1850s, it carried freight and passengers on rail cars until the early 1860s. By the time Watkins arrived the primary portage had been moved to the Washington bank of the river and the old road was used to carry lumber cut at the Eagle Creek Sawmill. The Eagle Creek Bridge (Plate 36) was also used by the herds of cattle and sheep being driven along the Columbia River Road towards Portland. The sign on the bridge declares a 25 cents per head toll on cattle, half price for sheep.

Watkins must have found this stretch of the river to his liking, for he made 18 stereographs in the immediate area. Many of these are scenic views with a more romantic atmosphere similar to that of *View on the Columbia* (Plate 35) or *Castle Rock, Columbia River* (Plate 20). The most idyllic of these is a stereograph titled *Moonlight on the Columbia* (No. 1287). Watkins did, in fact, make a number of stereographs of a pictorial nature all along the Columbia, photographs in direct contrast with the austere confrontation of the landscape which marks the majority of his mammoth views. *In the Orchard* (No. 1236), for example, made near the site of Cape Horn, shows a man standing in a group of fruit trees, eating an apple. *A Foggy Morning in the Cascades* (No. 1250), taken at the lower end of the Cascades, shows a fog-shrouded field of horses.

The stereograph *In Camp, ORR, Columbia River, Cascades* (No. 1288) made in the area of the Eagle Creek Sawmill is again a straightforward document of the subject. The photographer's dark tent is set up along the tracks, with the mammoth plate camera sitting on the ground next to the tree. The two men on the rail car are not identified, although it is likely that they are Joseph Bailey and John Stevenson, the two employees of the OSNC with whom Watkins is known to have had contact.

By the time Watkins finished his work in the Cascades area it was well into September. Boarding the steamboat at Upper Cascades—one of the two which made regular runs between there and Dalles City was the *Oneonta*—he made no photographs along the next 50-mile stretch of the Columbia. On September 28, 1867, the Dalles City newspaper *The Weekly Mountaineer* acknowledged the photographer's arrival.

> Mr. Watkins, a celebrated photographic artist from San Francisco, has been at work almost the entire summer taking views of the different places of note from the Cascades to Celilo. A few days ago we noticed his tent on the opposite side of the river among the rocks, where he was at work getting a view of our town and the Garrison. This, Mr. Watkins thinks, will make one of the finest pictures of any he has taken. The printing will not be done until his return to San Francisco.

Watkins' declaration of the sure success of the photograph *Dalles City from Rockland, Columbia River* (Plate 38), may have been made in his role as businessman, assuring the residents of Dalles City that the town portrait they would soon have the opportunity to purchase would be of high quality. The newspaper account also provides insight into the photographer's intent in making the picture. In this view Watkins' concern was clearly more than the town alone; he would not have included such a broad expanse of foreground had Dalles City been the actual subject of the picture. The wide angle of view of his lens is apparent here and the equal space given to the sky and the foreground rocks must be seen as a conscious compositional element. The stereograph corresponding to this view was made much closer, with the rail fence forming the immediate foreground.

From Dalles City Watkins traveled some 15 miles upstream by train along the Dalles and Celilo Railroad, another portage railroad run by the Oregon Steam Navigation Company as a part of their Columbia River monopoly. The portage bypassed a section of rapids which is now submerged by the waters behind The Dalles dam, completed in the 1950s.[18]

It has always been assumed that because Watkins does not appear in his photographs he did all the work himself rather than depending on assistants as other photographers often did. Internal evidence in the photograph *Mount Hood and The Dalles* (Plate 42) suggests that Watkins did have some degree of help from another person on his Columbia River trip. The stereograph which accompanies this view was taken from the ridge above the white building at the center of the photograph and shows neither the building nor the railroad tracks. On the tracks near the center of Plate 42 is the ghost image of a man who appears to be carrying a camera on a tripod. Because of the long exposure required for the negative, the man would not have appeared in the picture had he not stopped, perhaps to refer to Watkins for directions. The distance is too great for the stereograph to have been developed at the same dark tent location as the mammoth plate; the second man was probably going ahead to set up the camera at the other position.

The photograph Watkins made at Cape Horn, a 1000-foot rock promontory near Celilo (Plate 44) is the most remarkable of those he produced in Oregon, not for the importance of its subject but for the abstract planar strength of its composition. A corresponding stereograph was made from the same location but slightly closer, with the narrower angle of view of the stereo lenses centering on the tracks and the rock face and including none of the foreground water at the left of the mammoth view. It should be noted here that the two Cape Horns Watkins photographed are some distance apart, and that the duplication of names arises from their location on opposite banks of the river, the first Cape Horn in what is now Washington State (Plates 17, 18 and 48).

At Celilo Watkins made the last photographs of his 1867 trip, again centering on the Oregon Steam Navigation Company facilities (Plate 47). His return to Portland would have been relatively simple; the trip from Dalles City, including the transfer on the portage railroad, took only a day. Although he is not listed as a passenger on sailings before the end of 1867 it is likely that Watkins returned to San Francisco as he had come, on the *Oriflamme*. After spending more than three months away from his fledgling gallery he was surely anxious to return, to attend to his new business and to begin printing the negatives made in Oregon and along the Columbia River.

During the two or three years following the 1867 Oregon trip Watkins did not engage in extensive travel away from San Francisco, perhaps indicating that his gallery made demands on his time and that work from Yosemite and Oregon was continuing to sell well. Soon after his return, however, he sent a group of mammoth photographs from Yosemite to the Paris International Exposition. The Lawrence & Houseworth gallery, one of Watkins' major competitors in San Francisco, had received a medal from the Exposition judges in 1867 for a group of mammoth Yosemite pictures made by their photographer, C. L. Weed. After receiving the award Lawrence & Houseworth promptly had an engraving of the medal printed on the back of their stereo cards which advertised it as the only one presented for California views. The award and the stereocard advertisement seriously threatened Watkins' reputation as a photographer of the California landscape, but he managed to reestablish that identification by winning the same medal in 1868.[19] His friend, William Keith, made an engraving of the medal for the Yosemite Art Gallery stereocards, but apparently copied the Lawrence & Houseworth card rather than the actual medal. While Keith dated the award correctly in the advertisement, the roman numeral on the engraved medal was transcribed as MDCCCLXVII (1867).

In 1870 Watkins accompanied Clarence King and the U.S. Geological Survey during their travels in Northern California, and in 1871 he photographed the North Bloomfield Gravel Mines in Nevada County for potential buyers. Even though these trips were made for specific clients he was able to add to his expanding "Watkins' Pacific Coast" series of stereographs and prints. About this time he also began to acquire negatives from other photographers to issue under his own imprint, a common practice among photographers throughout the country which allowed them to build a larger catalogue of offerings without the time and expense of an expedition to distant places. The largest acquisition Watkins made was a set of more than 350 stereograph negatives by Sacramento photographer A. A. Hart which documented construction of the Central Pacific Railroad. In 1873 he also purchased an important set of negatives of the Modoc Wars from the Fort Jones, California, photographer, Louis Heller.

By 1872 Watkins' success was such that he was able to move his gallery to larger quarters at 22-26 Montgomery Street in San Francisco and began to look for additional ways to market his work. He produced a number of large presentation albums of his mammoth views, each measuring approximately 27½ x 24 inches, bound in leather with an oval-shaped piece of polished redwood set in the cover. His gold-toned albumen prints were glued to cardboard which had been printed with a rectangle of cream-colored ink just larger than the print. Titles were written beneath each photograph in a stylish hand and each album contained a two-color title page printed by letterpress. Three different albums were produced, each issued in a small edition: *Photographs of the Pacific Coast*, *Photographs of the Yosemite Valley*, and *Photographs of the Columbia River and Oregon*.

The albums bear the imprint of the Bartling & Kimball Company, San Francisco book binders who had their offices at the corner of Clay and Sansome. Since Bartling & Kimball advertised themselves not only as binders but as blank-book manufacturers it is likely that Watkins commissioned them to make a number of books and mounted the pictures within them himself. This is suggested by the fact that the book *Photographs of the Pacific Coast,* now in the Department of Special Collections at the Stanford University Library, has a number of blank pages which have the inked rectangle but show no indication that a print once there has become unmounted.

The lavishness of the albums and their bindings indicates that they were intended as items of import. The original purchaser of the album from which the reproductions in this book were made is not known, but the events surrounding the production of a similar 35-print album now housed in the Oregon State Library in Salem does provide an idea of the manner in which these albums were purchased and distributed.

By the early 1870s the Oregon Steam Navigation Company's control over transportation in the Northwest had increased and the national railroads, particularly the Northern Pacific, were anxious to gain control of the OSNC in order to complete their northern transcontinental route. In early 1872 the owners of the OSNC agreed to sell their holdings and the company president, Captain John C. Ainsworth, was sent east to negotiate the sale with Jay Cooke, who represented the Northern Pacific interests.[20] On his return trip to Portland Ainsworth passed through San Francisco where, on April 26, he noted in his diary that he "ordered [a] set of Columbia River views for Jay Cooke".[21] Cooke acknowledged the gift in a letter written to Ainsworth on May 21, 1872. "I shall be very thankful for the set of Columbia River views. I [will] make good use of all of these as there is much interest in regard to that wonderful country."[22]

Further correspondence from Cooke to Ainsworth does not reveal when the album was actually delivered, although it can be assumed that Watkins proceeded with the order rapidly. The Cooke album is of the same dimensions as the other *Columbia River and Oregon* albums, but contains 35 rather than 51 photographs. The leather cover is decorated not with polished redwood but with the gold-inlay inscription, "C. E. Watkins' Photographs of the Columbia River Presented by the Oregon Steam Navigation Company to Jay Cooke." A seal inside the cover again identifies Bartling & Kimball as the binders.

There is no record of previous purchases of the Columbia River photographs by Ainsworth or other officials of the Oregon Steam Navigation Company, but the selections Ainsworth made for this album confirm the OSNC interest in the gift. None of the Portland views were included, and only one each from the Oswego and Oregon City groups. The bulk of the photographs are those which illustrate the railroad and portage facilities to be acquired by the Northern Pacific. It should be noted here that a year after the sale was completed Jay Cooke's organization suffered financial failure as the country came under the grips of the economic depression of the 1870s. After a period of negotiation control of the OSNC returned to Portland interests.

Watkins' business seems initially to have thrived in its new location. The Yreka, California, *Journal,* reporting on Louis Heller's sale of the Modoc War pictures, told of "twenty women and a number of Chinamen being kept constantly at work" in the gallery.[23] In 1873 Watkins traveled with his painter friend, William Keith, to Utah along the tracks of the Central Pacific Railroad. They traveled in style, with one railroad car carrying their horses, wagon and supplies; another used as living quarters.[24] The cars may have been provided, as Turrill suggests, by the builder of the railroad, Collis P. Huntington, Watkins' old friend.[25] The fact of their use, however, indicates the extensive trappings required by a successful photographer in pursuit of new pictures for his expanding catalogue.

The economic depression which spurred the 1873 bankruptcy of Jay Cooke took its toll on the West Coast as well, affecting the market for less essential items such as photographs. It was disastrous for Watkins who, despite business successes in the early 1870s, had not completely recovered the expenses incurred in his move to the new gallery location. In 1876, for the first time in 11 years, the San Francisco city directory contained no notice of a Watkins photography gallery. I. W. Taber was listed as proprietor of the Yosemite Art Gallery at the 26 Montgomery Street address. Unfortunately, the specific circumstances of Watkins' bankruptcy have not been established. He had apparently borrowed money from Taber, an operator who had been associated with the Bradley and Rulofson gallery located next door to the Yosemite Art Gallery during the late 1860s. When his creditor requested payment, Watkins was forced to give up his gallery and its contents.

Watkins' life after his bankruptcy has not yet been thoroughly researched.[26] During the late 1870s he continued his work in photography, returning to Yosemite to make new negatives of the sites of his most popular views. He also explored new territory in the Comstock Lode around Virginia City, Nevada. In 1880 he established a gallery at 427 Montgomery Street and made a long trip through Southern California and Arizona.

He began to publish his post-1876 photographs as "Watkins' New Series", a series which included stereographs as well as prints made in a larger format he referred to as *boudoir* size, approximately 4¾ x 8 inches. He also continued to produce and publish photographs made with his mammoth plate camera. In advertisements after his bankruptcy Watkins publicly disowned his previous work, which was now being published by Taber under his own imprint, "A Taber Photograph", without giving credit to the photographer:

> Mr. Watkins cordially invites you to inspect his New Series of Views of the Pacific Coast from Mexico to Alaska, the Yosemite, Columbia River & Yellowstone Park. He is proud to say that his work is pronounced "the perfection of Landscape Photography," and nature is reproduced in his instantaneous pictures. He wishes particularly to state that he has no interest in his "old series" of views, now published by Mr. Taber, and to caution the public against spurious copies of his "new series" published by this party, the inferiority of which will be readily perceived by comparison with the originals.[27]

The manager of Watkins' San Francisco gallery while he traveled in Southern California was Frances Sneed, a woman he had met several years earlier in Nevada and whom he married in late 1880. They had two children, Julia and Collis. The letters he wrote to Frances during his travels reveal a new caution in the operation of his business as well as a desire to be back in San Francisco with his new wife.[28]

Travel was a necessary part of the life of an expeditionary photographer, however. Watkins made one, and possibly two trips to Oregon after his expedition in 1867. The first, in 1882, is well documented; the second, two years later, is not. On September 19, 1882, after spending some time in the Seattle area, Watkins wrote to his wife from Portland's Esmond Hotel.

> I never had the time seem so long to me on any trip that I ever made from home and I am not half done [with] my work. In fact, hardly commenced. It drags along awful slow between the smoke and the rain and the wind and as if the elements were not enough to sorry me a spark from an engine set fire to my tent and burned it half up, and it was the merest chance that it did not ruin the whole outfit. I was where I could not see it but some men working near called out to me and I got to it in time to prevent it doing any damage except to the tent. It took a couple of days to repair damage, and of course money.
>
> I expect to get through with the Puget Sound work in about ten days, and then I have all the Columbia River work to do and the Lord knows when I will get through with that.

Watkins' presence in Portland is confirmed by the list of

hotel arrivals published in the *Oregonian* on September 20. A display advertisement in the same issue of the paper announced the San Francisco Gallery of W. H. Towne at the corner of First and Morrison, the address of the Joseph Buchtel gallery. In an interview with Eugene Compton, Watkins' daughter Julia mentioned a young photographer named Towne whom Watkins had helped before he moved to Portland.[29] The San Francisco city directory lists William H. Towne as an operator for William Shew as early as 1873. In 1880 Towne moved to Portland, where he worked first with Frank Abell, another successful Oregon photographer, before going into partnership with Joseph Buchtel. By the early 1880s Buchtel had amassed a collection of some 30,000 negatives, a remarkable visual document of the growth of Portland and the surrounding area over a 20-year period. After thirty years in the West, however, Buchtel felt the desire to visit friends and relatives in the East. He made his trip, leaving his new partner, Towne, in charge of the gallery. Lacking Buchtel's sense of history Towne disposed of the old glass negatives and changed the business name to the San Francisco Gallery.[30]

As tragically intriguing as this episode is in a general sense, its significance here is that when Watkins arrived in Portland in 1882 he had an established contact with whom he could work. In the September 19th letter to his wife he mentions the need to finish his Puget Sound work before beginning on the Columbia River. It initially seems strange that Watkins would be in Portland with work still to be done 150 miles north. By this time, however, Watkins, like other photographers, was using commercially prepared dry plates rather than the older, more time-consuming wet plates.

The dry plates made it unnecessary to develop each exposure as it was made, but the quality of the image on the exposed plate deteriorated if development was not completed within a relatively short period of time. In Portland Watkins finished the processing of his Puget Sound negatives, work which was undoubtedly carried out in Towne's gallery.

On his 1882 trip Watkins again photographed along the Columbia River, this time traveling along the newly constructed railroad tracks on the Oregon bank of the river. He made a few photographs at the locations of the 1867 views but generally explored areas which he had either bypassed earlier, such as Oneonta Falls, or which had not existed 15 years before, such as the partially constructed locks at the Cascades. He traveled as far up the river as Dalles City and made a side trip up the Hood River to a point where he finally was able to photograph Mt. Hood at close range. There is a mammoth view of Mt. Hood in the collection of the Oregon Historical Society, but it has no markings which definitely attribute it to Watkins.

Photographs made on this trip were published as a part of the "New Series of Pacific Coast Views". The stereograph series, numbered beginning with E1, contains approximately 50 views, some of which were not added until after 1884. The greatest number of photographs Watkins made in 1882, however, were made with a larger camera. The published prints were 8⅜ x 12⅛ inches, mounted on boards 12¾ x 16½ inches. Forty-five of these were included in an album titled *Sun Sketches of Columbia River Scenery* which is in the collection of the Oregon Historical Society. The album was presented in 1884 to Julius L. Meier, Governor of Oregon, by J. Neilson Barry. It also carries the signature of C. H. Prescott, Treasurer of the Oregon Railroad and Transcontinental Company.

What is significant in this album is the inclusion of four prints which were obviously made from the mammoth negatives of the 1867 trip. It is clear that when I. W. Taber took over the Yosemite Art Gallery Watkins was able to retain some of his negatives. The four in the *Sun Sketches* album correspond to Plates 15, 18, 37 and 48 in this book. The Cape Horn photograph, which is identical to Plate 48, appears to be printed from a copy negative made from the earlier print. It is a smaller version of the original. The others, however, were printed from the full 18 x 22-inch negative and subsequently cut down to the smaller size. Since details of foliage and water level are identical they could not be from negatives made at the same locations fifteen years later. Of particular interest is the third photograph in the album, which is a vertical section cropped from the left side of *Cape Horn, Columbia River* (Plate 18). The composition of the new format image appears as purposefully balanced as the original.

Another album of photographs at the Oregon Historical Society places Watkins back in the Portland area in late December, 1884, although no other evidence has been discovered to confirm his presence there. The album contains 30 photographs made immediately after what the album calls the "Great Storm of the Winter of 1884-85". The prints, approximately 7 x 9½ inches but probably trimmed down from larger prints, are mounted on boards with printed titles. They are identified as part of "Watkins' New Series" and the address of the 427 Montgomery Street gallery is given. The album was bound by Meston & Digert, a Portland firm.

The photographs document the effects of an unusually heavy late-December snow storm along the railroad between Rooster Rock and Oneonta Falls, a distance of some ten miles. The first twelve pictures show the railroad crews clearing deep snow from the tracks while the rest are scenic views of the snow-covered Columbia River landscape. Boudoir-size prints, which were made from the same negatives as the album prints, were also published by Watkins, as were stereographs of the winter scenes.

In order for Watkins to have made these photographs he would have had to be in Portland for other reasons when the storm hit. There are, however, no other Oregon photographs extant which can be identified as having been made by him that year, nor is there published evidence such as newspaper notices or lists of hotel arrivals which would place him at the scene. Watkins did travel actively during this period, however. He ranged as far north as British Columbia and as far east as the Anaconda Copper Mines and Butte, Montana. The routes of these trips have not been confirmed and he may have been returning to San Francisco via Portland in 1884, seizing on the opportunity of the unexpected storm to add to his catalogue of photographs. It is also possible that these photographs were actually made by W. H. Towne and the negatives purchased by Watkins to publish under his own name.

During the late 1880s, his last active years as a photographer, Watkins photographed the Bakersfield, California, area, where he made some 700 views for the Kern County Land Company. In 1889 he opened a studio at 26 New Montgomery Street in San Francisco but maintained his family residence at 1249 Market Street. During the 1890s, however, as his eyesight began to fail, he was no longer able to work. His son, Collis, and Charles Turrill, his biographer, assisted in printing the negatives. Watkins' friend, Collis Huntington, arranged for the railroad to deed to the photographer a small ranch in Yolo County's Capay Valley, providing him with a place to retire. Despite his poor health, however, Watkins appears to have preferred to remain in San Francisco, although his wife and children did spend some time in the country.

In the spring of 1906 Watkins began negotiations with Stanford University for the purchase of his collection of negatives and prints. Tragically, his Market Street home, where the negatives were stored, was destroyed by the fire following the April 17 earthquake before the sale was completed. After another year in the city Watkins moved with his family to the ranch at Capay Valley. In January, 1910, blind and too ill for his family to care for him, Watkins was placed in the California State Hospital in Napa. He died there in 1916, at the age of 87.

NOTES

1. Watkins' middle name has been generally accepted as Emmons. There are indications however, that it may actually have been Eugene.
2. Details of Watkins' early life have been drawn primarily from the writings of three researchers whose work was published in the Fall, 1978, issue of *California History*. The three major articles of this important volume are "Before Yosemite Art Gallery: Watkins' Early Career" by Pauline Grenbeaux, "Watkins' Style and Technique in the Early Photographs" by Nanette Sexton and "Watkins—The Photographer as Publisher" by Peter Palmquist. Their contribution to this essay is gratefully acknowledged.
3. Charles B. Turrill, "An Early California Photographer: C.E. Watkins," *News Notes of California Libraries* 13 (January 1918), pp. 29-37. This article, material for which was accumulated during the last years of Watkins' life, contains many inaccuracies. As a primary source it must be used cautiously.
4. Earlier Watkins images do exist—daguerreotype landscapes and portraits in the carte-de-visite format—but the Mariposa photographs form the first significant group of prints.
5. Before the development, in the 1880s, of the halftone process for reproducing continuous tone illustrations it was necessary to make intaglio representations, such as wood-cuts or engravings, of a photographic image. These intaglios produced the actual printed impression. The photograph was used as a model and details were often changed by the engravers to make the illustration more "artistic".
6. Peter Palmquist's major article describing the work of this previously little-known photographer is to be published in the Fall, 1979, issue of *California History*.
7. Oliver Wendell Holmes, "Doings of the Sunbeam," *Atlantic Monthly* 12 (July 1863), pp. 7-8.
8. Turrill erroneously reports that Watkins made his first trip to Oregon in 1868, a claim repeated by a number of later writers. It is clear that Watkins was in Oregon in 1867; there is no evidence of an 1868 trip.
9. Theodosia Teal Goodman, "Early Oregon Daguerrotypers and Portrait Photographers", *Oregon Historical Quarterly* 49 (1948), pp. 30-49. This valuable article contains detailed information on several early photographers active in Oregon.
10. By way of comparison, the angle of view of a "normal" lens on a modern 35mm camera is approximately 45 degrees. A 28mm lens for a 35mm camera has an agle of view of some 76 degrees.
11. An anonymous photograph reproduced on page 66 of Weston Naef's book *Era of Exploration* shows Watkins' display at an 1870 exposition which was possibly held in Cleveland. The Portland and Oregon City panoramas are both shown framed as single units. A number of the single Columbia River and Oregon views are among the other framed mammoth plate prints Watkins exhibited there.
12. Watkins titled these photographs (Plates 11-14) *Oswego Iron Works*. While this is not incorrect, the proper name of the Oregon Iron Company, which was located in Oswego, is used throughout this volume.
13. Turrill, p. 30.
14. Watkins apparently published 57 mammoth views following his trip although he may have finished the expedition with more. Breakage enroute to San Francisco was certainly a possibility. He may have also decided that others did not meet his standards after the negatives were printed. The six mammoth views which were not a part of the 1872 presentation album, reproduced here, include the following:
    - the third panel of the Portland panoramic view
    - another view of the Oregon Iron Company
    - a frame-filling side view of the steam engine *S.G. Reed* taken in the engine switching yard shown in Plate 22.
    - the steamer *Oneonta* and the portage train at the Upper Cascades
    - a view on the Columbia River near Eagle Creek
    - a distant view of Mt. Hood from Sunset Hill, near Dalles City
15. Frank B. Gill, "Oregon's First Railway", *Oregon Historical Quarterly* 25 (September 1924), pp. 171-235.
16. T.F. Levens, *Freaks of Early History During the Early 50s and Later Down to the Present Time*. Undated 19th century manuscript remembrance in the collection of the Oregon Historical Society.
17. Weston J. Naef and James N. Wood, *Era of Exploration: The Rise of Landscape Photography in the American West, 1860-1865* (New York Graphic Society, 1975), pp. 26, 33, ff.
18. The rapids upstream from Dalles City was called The Dalles. In recent times the name of the town has been changed unofficially to The Dalles.
19. The events surrounding the awarding of the two medals have been subject to considerable discussion and confusion. In *Era of Exploration* Naef argues that some of the views attributed to Weed may have actually been taken by Watkins. Peter Palmquist's *California History* article on Weed (see note 6, above), makes a strong case for Weed's authorship.
20. Irene Lincoln Poppleton, "Oregon's First Monopoly," *Oregon Historical Quarterly* 9 (1908), p. 296.
21. John C. Ainsworth papers, Special Collections Division, University of Oregon Library.
22. John C. Ainsworth papers, Special Collections Division, University of Oregon Library.
23. Quoted in Peter Palmquist, "Watkins—The Photographer as Publisher", *California History* 57 (Fall, 1978), pp. 254-255.
24. Brother Cornelius, F.S.C., *Keith, Old Master of California*. (Putnams Sons, 1942). p. 78. Naef states in *Era of Exploration* that Keith also accompanied Watkins on his first Oregon trip. No evidence has been found to substantiate this claim.
25. Turrill, p. 36.
26. Information concerning Watkins' life in San Francisco after 1876 has again been drawn from the Fall, 1978, issue of *California History*.
27. Quoted by J. W. Johnson in "The Early Pacific Coast Photographs of Carleton E. Watkins," *Water Resources Center Archives, University of California, Berkeley* 8 (February, 1960). p. 10.
28. Watkins' letters are in the collection of the Bancroft Library, University of California, Berkeley.
29. Notes from this interview are also in the collection of the Bancroft Library.
30. Goodman, p. 46-47. Some years later Portland historian Fred Lockley attempted to salvage Buchtel's negatives from Balch's Gulch, in the hills above Portland, where they had been discarded in the early 1900s. Unfortunately, few of those recovered were in printable condition.

WATKINS ON THE COLUMBIA RIVER

AN ASCENDENCY OF ABSTRACTION

By Russ Anderson

By the outset of his photographic expedition to the Columbia River and Oregon in July of 1867, Carleton E. Watkins was a mature photographer. His technical and visual skills were acute and sensitive, honed to a fine sharpness during six years of landscape photography. With the publication of this book, which contains all 51 of his mammoth plate prints from the album *Photographs of the Columbia River and Oregon,* we are presented with a long overdue opportunity to re-evaluate the work of a photographer whose monumental artistic achievements are only now being fully appreciated. This album presents us with a unique critical perspective since the pictures were made over a relatively short time, from July to October of 1867. In that brief period Watkins exercised his capabilities to their fullest and we find an ascendency of abstraction in a body of work that is imaginative, powerful and complete.

Of the fifty-one mammoth plate albumen prints in the album, the forty-seven horizontal pictures are evidently presented in the sequence in which they were made. The four vertical photographs are placed out of sequence on the last pages for viewing convenience. The chronological order is largely substantiated by the attending negative numbers and the associated stereo views made at the same time.

Watkins' extensive use of the mammoth plate camera had begun six years earlier in Yosemite. The exacting and complex process of handling the 18 x 22-inch wet plate glass negatives in the field required the utmost attention to detail. Nevertheless, from the start, Watkins' technical skills had surpassed those of other users of the large format and by 1867 his technique was masterful. The overall impression that one gets from viewing prints of this size is that of grandeur and sweeping clarity; this format perfectly suited Watkins' landscape aesthetic.

In his travels up the Columbia River, Watkins was faced with a wide variety of potential subjects. He seems to have photographed most of the significant geological features and documented well the incursion of man in firmly rooted settlements and the growth of transportation and industry.

The landscape of the river changed dramatically in the course of his journey. Starting from a relatively flat expansive form, it develops gradually into a rich undulating countryside and then opens into stark dramatic vistas, barren of trees and punctuated by massive outcroppings of stone formation and rift etched by the river into the bed of the landscape. The seasonal changes from summer to autumn during his expedition are obscured by this significant change of landscape.

With landscape photographs of an excursionary nature, it is often difficult for the viewer to get beyond the intrinsic beauty of the subject itself. To come to a full appreciation of an artist's capabilities it can be helpful to examine the effect of some of the more formal characteristics of his work, for it is the formal qualities of an image which set it apart from mere evidential documentation. At times the landscape itself may be so overpowering as to obscure the photographer's individuality. The views of Yosemite Valley done by Watkins and others may reflect this to some extent. They are monumental images, not only in the refinement of their beauty but also in their depiction of one of the most intrinsically grand landscapes on the face of the earth. The Columbia River landscape, in contrast, is beautiful but less obviously dramatic and it is here that Watkins' preeminent excellence as a photographer becomes critically apparent.

Except in a strictly historical sense, the evidence of place provided to us by Watkins is far less important than the evidence his photographs provide of his genius as a picture maker. The appreciation of many 19th century images can sometimes be clouded by the historical weight they may carry. As the growth of the medium is unravelled by modern historians, judgments of a given photographer's central artistic concerns may sometimes be shaped by whichever portion of his work first comes to critical light. Certainly this was true of our estimation of artists such as Roger Fenton and P.H. Emerson. As we have been made aware recently of the refined achievements of their later work, we are now better able to comprehend their extensive abilities as artists. With Watkins the Yosemite pictures gained initial importance. With the present public emergence of these pictures, we discover a remarkable additional contribution, one which finds the photographer at the pinnacle of his visual inventiveness.

For those of us who spend a great deal of time looking at, thinking about and discussing photographs, historical and evidential associations are easily made. The documentary importance of the image becomes secondary to our own perception of a photograph's meaning as an image and the subjective feelings it evokes. Our association with the subject matter of an image, particularly one from which we are removed by more than one hundred years, must be changed considerably. So it is with these pictures by Watkins. Our appreciation of the photographer's ability to display clearly his understanding of a landscape and the effects of its inhabitants has been changed dramatically by the success and integrity of his visual statements. Watkins, in creating these images of a highly evidential nature, also created images of great intensity, and ordered that intensity in such a way as to harmoniously invite the viewer to explore the picture purely for its own sake. We in the 20th century are sensually attuned to the very intensity created here, and it is within our nature to seek pictures like these in which such qualities are so carefully and powerfully wrought.

Today, we may view the Oregon pictures as transitional steps from the profuse richness of the Yosemite work to the stark minimalism displayed in his Southern California and coastal views of the 1870s and 1880s. Watkins certainly played a very delicate balancing act in these pictures; his developing sense of abstraction is evident both in use of spatial forms and in tonality. In practical terms, there is less a sense of confinement than in the Yosemite pictures, but the landscape of the Columbia River is a more expansive one than that of the great valley with its cathedral-like and protected atmosphere. In

Oregon, Watkins softened the potential harshness of a direct confrontation with his principal subjects by stepping back and placing more space around the object. Certainly in some cases he was unable to get any closer, but because there were often fewer major features contained in a given field of view, the effectiveness of a given image depended largely on how he handled the empty or near-empty space around these features. At this Watkins was a master, and it is in these Oregon pictures that this matured vision is most evident. The *Oregon Iron Company at Oswego* (Plate 11), *Castle Rock, Columbia River* (Plate 19), *Passage of the Dalles, Columbia River* (Plate 43), and *Cape Horn near Celilo* (Plates 44 & 45) are the most striking examples. And while *Cape Horn, Columbia River* (Plate 17) and *View on the Columbia, Cascades* (Plate 35) contain elements which recall a more romantic and picturesque vision that existed in some of his Yosemite work, their compositions are made all the more powerful by the carefully controlled balance of negative space in the sky and water against a fundamental landscape.

His careful selection of vantage point, sometimes to the exclusion of direct depiction of a principal element of subject matter is most intriguing. The print *Oregon Iron Company at Oswego* (Plate 11) is illustrative of an attempt to gain tension between planes by the creation of negative and positive space in the foreground. If one assumes that Watkins could have moved closer by continuing around the bend to the right of the frame, then the interplay of the glassy river and the foreground inclusion becomes a vital clue to our understanding of Watkins' sense of two dimensional space.

Certainly the tension that can exist between negative and positive space is brought to its most extreme in *Cape Horn near Celilo* (Plate 44). There is some shared feeling currently that this photograph, viewed by today's standards, may be the single most beautiful photograph made in the 19th century. Here the spatial interplay is staggering, yet the directness of the confrontation and the subtle tonality of the print are held together in a tightly controlled balance of light and dark. We are invited directly into the image by the receding train tracks and rich tonal masses. Yet the carefully controlled spatial forms and accentuated lines hold us back to consider their perfect balance in a more planar respect. A closer vantage point would destroy that balance. This provocative image is a testimony to Watkins' mastery of the simple elements and their composition to form an abstract yet intensely exciting picture.

In this case the view may have been immediately evident to Watkins as he came upon the subject. It was likely he was traveling by train along the tracks in the picture. The images that directly precede Plate 44 in the album, and in time in all probability, show similar concerns that could lead us directly to this realization. *Mt. Hood and The Dalles, Columbia River,* (Plate 42) shows more vista, but we find similarities in the use of space. The balancing here plays strongly between the sky, the line of the horizon, and the diagonal formed by the mass of rock on the left. The brilliance of the light is subdued on the one hand by depth of tone on the left and the subtle middle tones on the right, but we are made aware of the intensity of the light by the highlighted building facade.

In *Passage of The Dalles, Columbia River* (Plate 43) the vertical elements are missing entirely. The spatial balance, left and right in the foreground, is accentuated here by a careful layering of tones receding to the horizon. Once again we are compelled to stand our ground and savor just what the artist has presented. The careful rendering of light on the foreground rock, forming a series of pleasing angles, leads us on to study the interlocking pattern of horizontal lines in the background. The linear minimal qualities exhibited here reflect Watkins' ability to use the landscape itself to best advantage, and the landscape was certainly more minimal at this stage in the journey. The maturity of his vision becomes evident. There is little attempt to make lyrical or classical statements, but instead to create a direct depiction of the inherent qualities of the landscape itself.

It is this kind of intensity coupled with austerity that can be so pleasing to us today as we view the masterpieces of the 19th century. Without doubt a number of Maxime DuCamp's views of Egypt, Roger Fenton's Crimean photographs and Gustave LeGray's seascapes come to mind as principle examples of this genre. But this kind of vision had certainly given way in Europe to a more idealized and lyrically stylistic viewpoint by 1860. In the American West, perhaps owing to the very nature of the landscape in which they worked, Timothy O'Sullivan and William Bell, Watkins and, to some extent, William Henry Jackson and A.J. Russell displayed these distinctly austere characteristics in their work with much more frequency.

In some of his more linear compositions Watkins was able to further demonstrate his heightened understanding of minimal elements. In their entirely evidential nature, the panoramas of the *City of Portland and the Willamette River* (Plates 1 & 2) and *Oregon City and Willamette Falls* (Plates 4, 5, & 6) can be seen to be examples of his care in composing these elements. (A third plate of the Portland panorama did exist but was probably lost or destroyed between 1867 and the printing of the plates for the album in the early 1870s.) In the Portland panorama upjutting tree stumps serve to accentuate the viewer's stance in relation to the city below in the foreground. The difficulty of obtaining a sense of depth in such a view is great, but Watkins manages quite well by placing the horizon in the middle of the frame and stretching it unbroken across the length of the picture, save for the diminished rise of Mt. St. Helens. There are actually two horizon lines here, one accented by the tree line just in front of the other less distinct range of hills. Some sense of aerial perspective is gained by the distant haze partially obscuring the line of hills. The careful layering of the foreground, river line and tree line carries us to the horizon with ease, and the blank sky serves to take us even further into the distance. These features, coupled with an expansive lateral view heightened by the unbroken linearity of the horizon, make the panorama all the more impressive.

In the Oregon City panorama, on the other hand, we are more confined by distance. Here an elegant foreground of rock and water undulates through the frame carrying the in-depth space to the opposite shore and a little beyond to where one's vision is stopped abruptly at the tree line. The effect of linearity is striking. It is once again carried from the extreme left to the extreme right with the same care exercised in the Portland panorama, only here the line is a gentle arc. Resting slightly below the middle of the frame, the down-turned arc is punctuated along its length in staccato rhythm by small buildings, by windows and boards on buildings, pier pilings, and windows on boats. Coupled with this is another line, an upturned arc, formed by the trees. The spatial interplay of the foreground masses complements these two somewhat complex but clearly defined lines.

The making of panoramas which hold together visually as these do is not an easy task. For those readers who are photographers, an attempt to make such a panorama in the same fashion might be a very instructive lesson in just how complex it can be. Nevertheless, Watkins succeeded beautifully. He thought enough of these two in particular to exhibit them made up as panoramas in at least one exposition in 1870.

In the course of his journey up the Columbia River the dramatic changes in the landscape and the variety of subject matter provided Watkins with an opportunity to exercise a fairly wide range of stylistic choices and interpretations. These vary from images that are classical in nature such as *Castle Rock, Columbia River* (Plate 19), through more romantic and lyrical styles as in *View on the Columbia, Cascades* (Plate 35), to very severe images exemplified by *Passage of The Dalles, Columbia River* (Plate 43).

More strikingly, even when faced with subjects of inherent romantic possibilities, he sometimes chose a breathtakingly primitive stance and refined the overall recording of that subject to its bare essentials. This can be most clearly seen in his handling of two of the three Multnomah Falls pictures. In

Plate 50 the vertical image is sharply divided down the middle of the frame by the falls. The viewer is given little in the way of depth perceiving devices, but rather is left to explore the picture randomly from a point suspended in space. The wholly abstract nature of the composition is held together by control of the tonalities. In Plate 51, however, a more classical approach is used. It provides us with a direct confrontation in the centering of the organic form of the falls surrounded by wispy foliage. The foreground of rocks, water and broken tree stumps, though pitifully barren, is delightfully highlighted into animation by the play of light on the mixed surfaces.

A similar example of Watkins' use of direct confrontation, pushing the reality of his subjects to the edge of abstraction, can be found in his treatment in *Castle Rock, Columbia River* (Plate 19). Here the simple linearity exists as a device to accentuate the upthrusting rock. The strong classical posture of the edifice is softened to some degree by the amount of space Watkins has chosen to place around it. It is obvious that he could have moved considerably closer to the rock, but he has chosen to hold his distance. The real abstraction lies here in his use of the ambiguous foreground. In this case we are not given the spatial clues that some suitably placed inclusion would have provided, but rather are left to survey the rock from some distance across a diminished landscape void of any singular point of interest. We are further held at bay by the separation of the rock from the sandbar by the glassy backwater. We are left to our own devices for viewing the monument, to wander randomly across the sandbar to gain perhaps a better view, but nevertheless withheld from actually getting close to the rock. So clearly has Watkins isolated the monolith from close scrutiny that we are left with the sense that if we could cross the water, the surrounding forest would still prevent our gaining a good view of the rock.

The isolation is again highlighted in the next photograph of Castle Rock (Plate 20), wherein a slightly romanticized and much more stylistic view is obtained. We are placed even further afield and made aware of the wilderness of forest and mass of river which prevents our access to the rock itself. We are given these two views of Castle Rock as we are later given three views of Multnomah Falls. In each view is embodied a specific treatment by the photographer so as to enhance our understanding of a specific characteristic of the subject, but at the same time Watkins has varied the stylistic choices he has made to depict that subject.

In dealing with the architectural subjects in the album, we find that the role played by stylistic choices may be less obvious. Traditionally, the photographic treatment of architecture has either been one of direct confrontation or oblique romanticism. Watkins has generally chosen a middle ground, blending the architecture into the landscape without overt emphasis of either feature. Where he has chosen to deviate from this more gentle treatment the results are remarkably refined.

Of interest in this regard is the photograph *Oregon Iron Company at Oswego* (Plate 14). Perhaps to illustrate the engineering significance of the pipe joining the two buildings, Watkins has chosen to frame the main building to the extreme right of the image. Its stature is accentuated by comparison with the men standing next to it and the smaller structures on the left. This juxtaposition, coupled with an extended foreground and the rise of the building's tower above the horizon almost to the top of the frame, serves to emphasize its massive qualities. He handles this subject almost as he would have handled some natural formation in Yosemite, but here the spatial interplay of the distinct geometric forms and lines is the decisive key to picture. The vantage point Watkins has chosen makes full use of the various pleasing angles to enhance the composition. His careful orchestration of the vertical and diagonal lines brings harmony to a picture that could have easily been confused and cluttered.

In his approach to the *Flour and Woolen Mills, Oregon City* (Plate 10), Watkins also makes use of angles, but here it is the overall triangle formed by the buildings and the boat. One's vision diverges outwardly from the center, stopping to examine the fine detail of the structures before proceeding to the landscape beyond. Watkins does not subdue the everpresent landscape but neither does he allow it to encroach upon his delicate rendering of these simple but elegant buildings. One's attention perpetually returns to them for further scrutiny.

Watkins' ability to clarify the intrinsic characteristics of his subjects in varying stylistic motifs with apparent ease demonstrates a photographic vision of considerable skill and, in some cases, identifiable eccentricity. That Watkins was both skillful and eccentric there can be no doubt.

Consider for a moment an important aspect of this eccentricity which can be seen to play a pivotal role in Watkins' success as a picture maker. That is his predominating use of innovative and sometimes outlandish foreground elements as focal points or planes of reference in his pictures. In the Yosemite pictures made between 1861 and 1866, the use of the foreground to add perspective and a sense of scale was decisively important to his images. In some cases the determination to use these elements as he did was more out of necessity than choice. The confined environment of Yosemite Valley provided little room for the photographer to work free of foreground inclusions. In addition, Watkins had, by the early 1860s, become a highly competent stereograph maker. In the stereograph the skillful use of the foreground elements was essential to provide the viewer with spatial steps into the image. But most workers in stereo did not transfer such foreground usage to larger formats. Certainly, C.L. Weed and Eadweard Muybridge, in their large views of Yosemite, were not nearly so eccentric as Watkins in foreground delineation.

In the Columbia River pictures Watkins' diverse use of the foreground plane is a powerful tool. By the use of distinct objects, masses of uninterrupted surface or both, he repeatedly delights the eye with planar configurations, depth creating devices and ambiguous inclusions. These create not only spatial depth by drawing the viewer into the image, but also sometimes serve as vehicles for interesting visual excursions across the picture plane. The foreground in *Castle Rock, Columbia River* (Plate 19) is illustrative of this, as previously pointed out. More significantly, we are made aware of Watkins' superb sensitivity in the structuring of foreground elements throughout the Oregon pictures.

It would seem that another unusual stylistic tool, learned in earlier years, was used to his great advantage in Oregon. That is the placement of the dominant mass to one side of the frame, or perhaps in a corner or extreme foreground. In Yosemite this may have been necessary, once again owing to the confined environment. In order to accentuate a sense of depth behind the objects there, it was imperative for Watkins to treat his subjects with this off-center positioning. But in Oregon, where the vistas were more readily accessible, this off-center placement becomes a powerful stylistic tool. It occurs in more than twenty of the plates, which seems to indicate Watkins' preference for this kind of positioning. One would suspect, without actually examining the plates, that such structuring would give rise to an overly romanticized viewpoint. In fact, we can see that Watkins has clearly managed to avoid this and move toward abstraction. Throughout the body of work, we see continuing attempts to simplify the structure of his pictures, to boil the information contained in the landscape down to the bare essentials.

Compositonally, the power of these pictures is undeniable. Add to this the sumptuous richness obtained by Watkins in his mammoth plate gold-toned albumen prints and the effect is magnificent. The beautiful tonalities created here are testimony to the excellence of this early process as well as to Watkins' rigorous attention to technique. The long tonal scale serves to make the pictures all the more inviting. The highlights are brilliant yet finely detailed, and this detail carries all the way through the scale, down to the warm deep shadows. The quality of aerial perspective, that is, the well defined layering of tone from dark to light as we proceed into the distance, is exquisite.

This, coupled with the lavish, velvety deep tones gives a tactile sensuousness to the prints which draws the viewer into the images. Such luxuriant tonality serves to elevate the viewer's experience of the print as an object. Thus presented the prints radiate a presence of their own, adding yet another dimension to Watkins' genius.

The various stylistic choices and interpretations Watkins has made in the execution of the pictures in this album are direct evidence of his ordering of the landscape into some well-defined statement. How large a role these choices and interpretations play in the actual sequencing of the prints in the album is unclear. That the sequencing is different in the stereo views and in other albums raises the possibility of a conscious aesthetic sequencing. However, it is more likely that the progression represents a sequence of travel and that Watkins worked within that chronological framework in arranging the prints for the album. Viewed as a whole, the body of photographs is a substantial and provocative work. It is a fine and sensitive statement about the landscape of the Columbia River, but more importantly it represents a statement of the power that Watkins was able to bring to his images.

We find that any individual picture from the album will take on a separate life of its own. In each is embodied a seminal assertion of Watkins' power to generate emotive form complete in its own arrangement. Even the individual plates of the panoramas hold together visually when viewed singly.

That Watkins had achieved the highest levels of his vision during his trip to the Columbia River and Oregon, there can be no doubt. Each visual statement is carefully considered. Each vantage point is chosen to delineate a specific aspect of subject. As we view the album, looking for the key to open Watkins' vision to our understanding, we find that the key lies in the clarity of each individual statement as a separate entity.

Photographers tend not to create singular masterpieces, but rather unfold their masterful creations in bodies of work that reiterate a specific concept. For Watkins the concept was his perception of the landscape, and so acute was that perception that he did create individual masterpieces.

In viewing this album in relation to earlier and later work by Watkins, the pivotal role these pictures play is immediately apparent. We find the essence of what he had learned in the earlier Yosemite work brought to perfection here. At the same time he struck out in new directions that he would continue to explore for many years to come. As historians continue to study the career of this remarkable photographer and place into perspective his outstanding contribution to the medium, the Columbia River and Oregon pictures will play an important, if not decisive, role in that assessment.

Moreover, what Watkins created and compiled for us in this album is an extraordinary legacy. It contains all of the qualities that a man of perceptive genius may share with us. It adds a profound acquisition to our visual experience and provides provocative insight into the abstract and inventive vision of Carleton Watkins.

PHOTOGRAPHS

OF THE

COLUMBIA RIVER

AND OREGON.

BY

C. E. WATKINS,

Nos. 22 and 26 MONTGOMERY STREET,

SAN FRANCISCO.

Plate 1. City of Portland and the Willamette River

Plate 2.   City of Portland and the Willamette River

Plate 3. Oregon City

Plate 4. Oregon City and Willamette Falls

Plate 5. Oregon City and Willamette Falls

Plate 6.   Oregon City and Willamette Falls

Plate 7.   Willamette Falls, Oregon City

Plate 8. Willamette Falls, Oregon City

Plate 9.   Willamette Falls, Oregon City

Plate 10.   Flour and Woolen Mills, Oregon City

Plate 11.   Oregon Iron Company at Oswego, Willamette River

Plate 12.   Oregon Iron Company at Oswego, Willamette River

Plate 13.   Oregon Iron Company at Oswego, Willamette River

Plate 14.   Oregon Iron Company at Oswego

Plate 15. Mt. Hood from near Vancouver

Plate 16. Rooster Rock, Columbia River

Plate 17. Cape Horn, Columbia River

Plate 18. Cape Horn, Columbia River

Plate 19.   Castle Rock, Columbia River

Plate 20.   Castle Rock, Columbia River

Plate 21. Steamer *Cascade* at the Lower Landing, Columbia River

Plate 22.   Oregon Steam Navigation Company Works, Columbia River

Plate 23. The Garrison, Columbia River

Plate 24. The Middle Landing from the Oregon Side

Plate 25. **The Middle Block House**, Columbia River

Plate 26.   View from the Middle Block House, Columbia River

Plate 27. Ruins of the High Bridge, Columbia River

Plate 28. Upper Cascades, Columbia River

Plate 29.   The Rapids from the Block House, Cascades

Plate 30. The Rapids, Indian Block House, Cascades

Plate 31.   Islands in the Columbia, Upper Cascades

Plate 32.   Islands in the Columbia, Upper Cascades

Plate 33. Islands in the Columbia, Upper Cascades

Plate 34. **Upper Cascades** from the Oregon Side

Plate 35. View on the Columbia, Cascades

Plate 36. Eagle Creek, Columbia River

Plate 37. Tooth Bridge, Columbia River

Plate 38. Dalles City from Rockland, Columbia River

Plate 39. Mt. Adams from Sunset Hill, Dalles City

Plate 40.   Oregon Steam Navigation Company Works, Dalles City, Columbia River

Plate 41. Dalles City from the East, Columbia River

Plate 42. Mt. Hood and The Dalles, Columbia River

Plate 43.   The Passage of The Dalles, Columbia River

Plate 44.   Cape Horn near Celilo

Plate 45.   Cape Horn near Celilo

Plate 46. Tum Water, Columbia River

Plate 47.   Celilo

Plate 48. Cape Horn, Columbia River

Plate 49.   Multnomah Falls, Columbia River

Plate 50.   Multnomah Falls, Columbia River

Plate 51.   Lower Multnomah Falls, Columbia River

THE FRIENDS OF PHOTOGRAPHY

The Friends of Photography, founded in 1967, is a not-for-profit organization actively involved in the support and encouragement of creative photography. Over the years The Friends has built a network of contact and interchange between artists, historians, critics, students and the public. The programs of The Friends include publications, grants and awards to photographers, exhibitions, workshops, lectures and critical inquiry. The publications are devoted to the presentation of contemporary photographers' work as well as to the history and criticism of the medium. Membership is open to everyone. Address inquiries to The Friends of Photography, P.O. Box 239, Carmel, California 93921.

COLOPHON

Type: Garamond
Paper: Warren's Lustro Offset Enamel, 100 lb., cream, dull
Negatives: Hell DC300B laser scanner, 280 line

Printing: Gardner/Fulmer Lithograph, Buena Park
Typography: Instant Type, Monterey